CW00863452

# A Short Life
# on the
# Ocean Wave

**Also by the author:**

*I'll Give It Six Months*
A delightful and humorous Memoir

*Travels with My Appetite*
His take on travel and food

*With Apologies to Pam*
A book of Poems and Limericks

# A Short Life on the Ocean Wave

## A Memoir of Merchant Navy Days

Robert Howe

Copyright © 2019 Robert Howe

All rights reserved, including the right to reproduce this book, or portions thereof, in any form. No part of this text may be reproduced, transmitted, downloaded, decompiled, reverse engineered, or stored in any form, or introduced into any information storage and retrieval system in any form or by any means, whether electronic or mechanical, without the express written permission of the author.

The views expressed in this work are solely those of the author and do not necessarily reflect the views of the publisher, and the publisher hereby disclaims any responsibility for them.

ISBN: 978-0-244-77024-2


PublishNation
www.publishnation.co.uk

# Dedication and Thanks

To all the crews and shipmates I sailed with for their great camaraderie and the experiences we shared.

One must remember that memory dims with age so if I have some of the places and names not quite as they are, I apologise.

My thanks go to the anonymous Photographers whose photographs I may have used and Linda Fraser-Webb who diligently proof reads my rough drafts and turns them into readable copy.

# Contents

# Introduction

Many very famous writers have disagreed with the statement "write what you know" but such brilliant authors as Ernest Hemmingway have said that this is the way to go. He once said that he would write a book on each of the things he knew and I totally agree with this. Imagination is, of course, massively important but for factual writing nothing can beat personal experience. As I know a little about a lot and a lot about nothing I decided to write about something I did know a little about, The Merchant Navy. My service in the Merchant Marine started on 3rd May 1961 and finished on 4TH Sept 1962 and although quite short was extremely character forming, it was my University of Life and one of the best things I ever did. In that short space of time I had been around the world, met some very interesting people and had many unforgettable experiences.

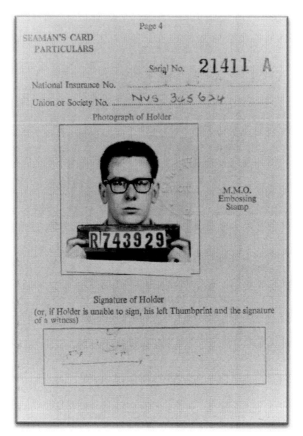

Page 4

SEAMAN'S CARD
PARTICULARS

Serial No. **21411 A**

National Insurance No. ................................

Union or Society No. ....... NVS 345624

Photograph of Holder

R743929

M.M.O.
Embossing
Stamp

Signature of Holder
(or, if Holder is unable to sign, his left Thumbprint and the signature of a witness)

*No, it's not a police suspect photo,
just my seaman's card or ID/Passport*

\* \* \*

The journey begins

# Chapter 1

## From Soho to The Isle of Dogs

In 1961 I was quite happily working for Edward Withers of Wardour Street as a violin restorer and repairer. I liked the work and Soho in the fifties was a really interesting place to work but felt that I needed to broaden my horizons.

Having missed National Conscription by about nine months, much to my father's disgust, I was beginning to realise that I had missed out on foreign travel and other experiences. I had an interest in photography at the time so I thought that the Royal Airforce would love to have me as an Aerial Photographer. Can't recall where I obtained the application documents but a short time after posting them I received instructions on where to report for the entry test and medical. A week or so later I was sitting in a waiting room with several other hopefuls waiting to see the Airforce Doctor. As I had applied for a job involving flying, special attention was paid to my eyesight as I was somewhat short sighted but afterwards I was told to await joining instructions. During that period, before I received the letter, my head was filled with images of me in a smart RAF uniform driving an open-top sports car a with a beautiful girl beside me. Alas that was not to be, a week later I got the letter but it was to inform me that my eyesight wasn't up to flying duties and I couldn't become a flying David Bailey, however I could join as part of the catering section. Chefs were not the celebrities they are today so after some thought I declined their kind offer. This surely was the shortest stint in the RAF but their loss was the Merchant Navy's gain.

I was still determined to see a bit more of the world so wrote several letters to various shipping lines with offices in the city of London. I must say most replied, amongst which was the Union Castle line, my sister had married years before and emigrated to South Africa and Union Castle sailed to SA so the choice was made easy. I attended an appointment somewhere in the city and before long was in front of the company's Doctor. This was the same routine as before but I recall for the first time in my life I was required to drop my trousers and cough! Coughing didn't seem to be a requirement in the RAF.

# Union-Castle Line
### TO SOUTH & EAST AFRICA.

## ROYAL EAST AFRICAN STEAMSHIP SERVICE

### Monthly via the Suez Canal, for

Mombasa, Zanzibar, Mozambique, Porto Amelia, Chinde, Beira, Lourenço Marques, and Natal ;
calling at
Gibraltar, Marseilles, Naples, Port Said, Suez, Port Sudan and Aden.

### Weekly via the West Coast, for

Cape Colony, Natal, Lourenço Marques, Beira, East Africa, and Mauritius ; calling at
Madeira, Las Palmas, Ascension, St. Helena, and Lobito Bay.

## Tours round Africa by Union-Castle Steamers

REDUCED FARES DURING JUNE, JULY, AND AUGUST TO CAPE TOWN AND NATAL.

Apply to
THE HEAD OFFICES OF THE COMPANY,
3 & 4 FENCHURCH STREET, LONDON, E.C.
to the Branch Offices at Cape Town, Lourenço Marques, Port Elizabeth, East London, Durban, Johannesburg ; or to the Company's Agents at the East African Ports.

From the company's offices I was sent to what I remember as a Seaman's Employment Centre where I was issued with a seaman's ID book/passport and a discharge book. Sun, Sea and South Africa here I come.

# Chapter 2

## The RAF's loss is the Merchant Navy's gain

My joining instructions arrived and I was told I was to be an Assistant Steward and should report to the Chief Steward on the Warwick Castle ship, currently berthed in the London Victoria docks.

The Victoria Docks was the oldest part of the Royal Docks complex, at the time the largest body of enclosed water in the world. In the fifties and sixties, the Port of London was at its peak but the development of larger ships and containerisation heralded in the closure of Victoria Docks in 1981. In the same year the Government formed the London Docklands Development Corporation and the London City Airport now stands on the former King George V dock site.

This was an important time for me, a complete life style change without the support of my family who I wouldn't see for six weeks. To mark the occasion my Dad took the day off to accompany me to the ship and at the dock gates shook my hand which was the first time ever he had done so. I found the ship and met the Chief Steward who informed me that the ship wasn't due to sail for a further three days. When I returned home that evening my mother immediately thought that I had been thrown out of the Navy on my first day. I spent the next three days acquiring some uniform and learning what a terrible mistake I had made. My previous employment had no physical work involved and after eight hours I got to go home. I learnt with increasing dread that my day with the Navy would start at 06.00hrs when I was required to clean a section of inside decking. This would be followed by humping supplies from the lower stores to the bars and restaurants, after which I was free to grab a quick breakfast (I never did find the time) before showering and changing into uniform and serving the passengers breakfast. Well I thought that wasn't so bad, at least I had the rest of the day to recover! Stupid boy, lunch began at 12.00hrs and after that the passengers (I hadn't seen one yet but already hated them) expected Beef Tea on deck in the winter or ice cream in the hot weather in the afternoon. Then all the time before dinner, which was served at 19.00hrs to 22.00hrs, was yours to clean shoes, press the uniform or just pass out.

*The London Docks in the 60s*

*MS Warwick Castle*

# Chapter 3

## Union Castle Line

The Union Castle shipping line operated a fleet of ships that sailed between Europe and Africa from 1900 to 1977. It was formed from a merger between The Union Line and the Castle Shipping Line. The newly formed company named most of their ships using the suffix "Castle" with very distinctive lavender hulls and red funnels topped with black. They plied the route round Africa calling at some twenty ports on the six-week voyage.

My first ship was built in 1938 as the Pretoria Castle, it became HMS Warwick Castle when it was recommissioned by the Royal Navy and used as a troop carrier during the second world war. At 08.44 hrs on 14th November 1942 the Warwick Castle, while in convoy, was hit by a torpedo from the German U-413 boat some 200 hundred miles off the Portuguese coast. The U-boat fired two torpedoes and the ship sank with a loss of 62 crew and 34 service personnel. The remainder of the crew and passengers were picked up by HMS Achates and the merchant ship Leinster and landed at Greenock. Sadly, the Achates itself was sunk on 31st December 1942 by the German cruiser, Admiral Hipper with the loss of 113 men.

Being born in August 1942 I am aware that I was alive when both these ships were sunk and I am always thankful that my own father, Robert, who served in the Royal Artillery during the war, came out of it safely unlike those poor sailors.

Ocean liners were vital in supporting the Military operations during the war. Massive numbers of troops and equipment were needed to be transported over vast distances and some of the passenger liners were the fastest means of doing that. With the threat of submarine attack speed was a big defence. Some of the ships requisitioned were used as troop carriers while others were armed and used against the enemy's merchant fleet. A few of the merchant ships were equipped as hospital ships to treat injured soldiers and to bring them home. Passenger ships were already equipped to carry large numbers and had all the facilities to do so but when converted to military use they were stripped back to the bare minimum to carry hundreds more. Camouflage played a big part in converting the vessels and the Warwick Castle was decked out in a dismal brown colour. Ships that survived the war, many did not, were returned to their former glory and went back to service, the Warwick Castle was one.

*The 1st Warwick Castle ready for war service*

# Chapter 4

## The First Landfall

The ship sailed and I began to realise that one; I was not cut out to be a steward and two; I was definitely not going to be a very good sailor. Looking back the ship was probably quite stable going through the English Channel but to me, having to ferry plates of food to real passengers, it was rolling dramatically. The old hands kept assuring me that I would soon find my sea legs but I never really did. The other gem of wisdom the old sea dogs liked to give new lads like me was "wait until we hit the Bay of Biscay". The Bay of Biscay lies off the western coast of France and the northern coast of Spain and was well known for its rough seas and violent storms due to its exposure to the Atlantic Ocean.

Two days later we were in that fearful bay but on this occasion, it was as calm as a mill pond and I had indeed began to acquire the semblance of sea legs. It was heartening to know that Admiral Horatio Nelson suffered from seasickness and occasionally struggled with life at sea. In a letter he wrote to his nephew, the Earl of Camden, who left the navy because of seasickness just a few months after joining HMS Victory in 1804, he said "I am ill every time it blows and nothing but my enthusiastic love for the profession keeps me one hour at sea". So, I was in very good company.

*A magnificent sight of my first port.*

I was now looking forward to our first port of call and my very first foreign country, Gibraltar. Sadly, I was scheduled to be on duty during the short stay so was unable to go ashore but I will never forget my first glimpse of this magnificent sight. Bathed in sunlight with the cable car reaching the top of the Rock it looked wonderful and I was sorry I couldn't step ashore. However, since that memorable day I have been to "Gib" five times.

Gibraltar has own language, Llanito, it's a bizarre mix of Andalusian Spanish and English with a bit of Portuguese and some Maltese words, words of Genoese dialect and even some of Hebrew origin. The locals tend to switch languages mid-sentence making it impossible for English or Spanish speakers to understand.

I was told that Gibraltar was the place to stock up on essentials, like alcohol. Although cigarettes could be bought at the crew stores, drink on-board was a definite no, no. However, our Master at Arms, who was an ex police officer, had an eye like an eagle and was also reputed to be able to smell alcohol through an un-opened glass bottle. It was a mystery as to where all the confiscated booze went to, suffice it to say that our Master always seemed in a good mood!

In those days the Master at Arms acted as the Police on board ship, his duties were to control the crew as well as the passengers and to stop and investigate any crime. The original job of the Master of Arms was to teach sailors the art of fighting with swords and small arms but in my days in the Navy it seems that his main job was to stop the sailors fighting each other.

# Chapter 5

## Bars, Dhows and a Canal

The itinerary for the round Africa voyage was quite full and called at some vey exotic places, this, at a time before packaged holidays came on the scene and was amazing for a nineteen-year-old who hadn't been out of the UK before. Ports visited: - Gibraltar - Genoa - Port Suez - Aden - Port Said - Mombasa - Dar-es-Salaam - Lourenco Marques - Beira - Cape Town - Port Elizabeth - East London - Durban - St. Helena – Ascension - Madeira - Les Palmas.

I may have missed out on Gibraltar but I aimed to catch up in Genoa and with the night off, I certainly did. Mention Genoa to any Merchant or Royal Navy seaman and you may well see a smile at the corners of their mouths, the place was jumping. Under the guidance of two stewards that had sampled the delights of the city many times I headed off to the notorious street of bars known as "The Dirty Mile". First up was The Zanzibar followed by The Atlantic Bar and then my favourite The Black Cat. To describe that evening as astonishing would not be doing it justice, the sights, sounds and smells all new to me were unforgettable. The bars were packed with crews from all over the world, a few of the more adventurous and brave passengers and loads of ladies of the night. I seem to remember getting back to the ship just in time to scrub my patch of deck and I think it took about three days before the smile went from my face, a great night.

After the excitement of Genoa came a few days at sea before our next port of call, Port Said at the mouth of the Suez Canal.

Suez Canal was completed in 1869 after a French engineer, Ferdinand de Lesseps persuaded the Egyptian viceroy to support the project. Construction started in 1859 and took ten years to complete at a cost of £75 million. In 1875 Egypt sold its shares to the United Kingdom and in 1888 an international convention made the canal available to all nations.

Shortly thereafter, conflicts began to arise over use and control of the Suez Canal. In 1936 for example, the U.K. was given the right to maintain military forces in the Suez Canal Zone and control entry points. In 1954, Egypt and the U.K. signed a seven-year contract that resulted in the withdrawal of British forces from the canal area and allowed Egypt to take control of the former British installations. In addition, with the creation of Israel in 1948, the Egyptian government prohibited the use of the canal by ships coming and going from that country. When Israel invaded Egypt and two days later Britain and France followed on grounds that passage through the canal should be free. In retaliation, Egypt blocked the canal by intentionally sinking 40 ships. These events were known as the Suez Crisis.

The Suez Canal can accommodate ships with a 210,000 tons deadweight. Most of the Canal is not wide enough for two ships to pass side by side and to accommodate this, there is one shipping lane and several passing bays where ships can wait for others to pass. The Canal has no locks because the Mediterranean Sea and the Red Sea's Gulf of Suez have approximately the same water level. It takes around 11 to 16 hours to pass through the canal and ships must travel at a low speed to prevent erosion of the canal's banks by the ships' waves.

I remember that when we were passed through the canal there were large groups of men working on the sides, clearing and digging. I got the impression that they may have been prisoners on a working party but I may be wrong. As we slowly passed some of the men lifted their gallibayas to expose themselves to our lady passengers, the sound of camera shutters was deafening. When we reached Port Suez and anchored, the ship was surrounded by small dhows trying to sell all manner of souvenirs including bottles of a Scottish brand of whisky. The old hands advised not to send our money down in the baskets they threw up but there's always one. After he paid and was hailing his bottle of whisky up; the trader was furiously rowing to the dock and of course the whisky was cold tea. A deck hand who witnessed this quickly got a water hose out and as the trader was departing the deck hand sprayed a powerful jet of water into his boat.

He made it to the shore but not before we saw all his souvenirs floating away.

After I left the Merchant Navy I worked with a guy that had been part of the British forces to invade Egypt during the Suez crisis. He tells the story that when he and the landing party were in the landing craft going on the attack the regulars and NCOs (he was on his National Service) were going around saying things like "good luck lads some of us may not be going home etc" and naturedly he was near to soiling his combat trousers. When the ramp went down he was faced not with hordes of fighting Egyptians but groups of traders trying to sell the invading forces dubious bottles of whisky and some very naughty photographs.

Next came the Port of Aden. Aden became the capital of the new People's Republic of South Yemen in 1970 and is now far from the scruffy but fairly safe place I remember. I have no idea why this was so but Aden was the place the crew went ashore to buy "boxer shorts" For the equivalent of about 15p each you could get them in very loud prints unavailable anywhere else.

# Chapter 6

## Magnificent Africa

*Mombasa*

Mombasa was considered one of the favourite ports by most of the crew and I had many a great night out there. The day always seemed to follow the same enjoyable pattern. After serving breakfast, a shower and change into a pair of shorts and flip-flops (in those days I seemed to live in white canvas uniform shoes or flip-flops), then a short taxi ride to the

Mombasa Seaman's Mission where you could have a few Tuskers beers and a swim in the pool or just relax for a few hours before you hit the town. And hit the town you did; I seem to remember eating a lot of grilled sweetcorn and skewers of unidentifiable meat cooked on an oil drum brazier. All this and much more went on in front of the Regal Cinema. A good friend today was, around that time, a Mombasa customs officer, and when the Regal Cinema is mentioned he just rolls his eyes and says, "not me, Bobby." I recall on one such outing when we were taken to a newly opened nightclub called the Dolphin Club where many G&Ts and much beer was consumed—I actually drank pink gins in those days but can't think why—it seemed to be the sensible thing to do to take off all our clothes and go for a swim in the pool. I don't remember what time I decided to walk back to the ship but I do remember waking up lying in a storm drain at about five o'clock in the morning with several little African kids pointing and laughing their little heads off. It was while the ship was docked in Mombasa that the purser's office organised a fishing competition for the crew. The dock was in deep water so a variety of fish was expected in the catch. However, no one expected what was pulled from the Indian Ocean in the late afternoon: a metre-and-a-half bull shark (*Carcharhinus leucas*). The bull shark is also known as the Zambezi shark and is considered one of the most dangerous sharks in the world since this species has made many attacks on humans. As you would expect, there was quite a bit of commotion going on as the shark was thrashing and snapping about on the deck and no one was prepared to throw it back or kill it. Someone suggested that it would fetch good money in the local market in the morning and that sealed its fate. One of the bosuns brought the discussion to a halt when, with the aid of a large sledge hammer, he despatched the shark. There was a twist to this story: when the two seaman who caught the shark went to collect it from the deck the next morning, it had vanished. Rumours were rife, but the most plausible was that it had been spirited away by some of the locals who had been taken on to paint some of the ship, leaving two very angry members of the crew.

*The flying Angel Seamans Mission Mombasa*

Many years later I returned to Mombasa for a holiday and had promised my friend, the former customs officer, to visit the Arab quarter to buy him some Paan. Paan, also called betel leaf, is a leaf used to make an Indian after-dinner mouth freshener and digestive. Fennel seeds, coconut flakes, cardamom powder, chopped betel and other spices are rolled in the leaf and chewed. Being born in Kenya he swore that the betel leaves from that country were far superior than any others and he could not get any in the UK. I got the hotel I was staying at to let me have a driver and go in the hotel's mini bus, had I known what would happen I would never have left the hotel's compound. The whole place was extremely seedy, certainly not what I remembered but we found a small Asian shop and I went in to buy the Paan. When I came out some ten minutes later I found that a drug addict, high on something, had taken a dislike to the mini bus and smashed the back window in with an iron bar. My poor wife who I had left in the "safety" of the bus was terrified and the driver wasn't much better. When we got back to the hotel the driver was in deep trouble for taking us to this very dangerous area and I had to plead with the hotel manager for the man's job. Very sad to see the city sink so low, I dread to think of the consequences to sleeping it off in a ditch now.

# Chapter 7

## Dar es Salaam and the Spice Island

Zanzibar was a fascinating place to visit, Stone Town with its winding lanes and Mosques was the centre of the slave trade being one of the largest slave ports in the Indian Ocean. The slave traders, bribed chiefs, pillaged and frequently kidnapped to meet the high demand for slaves.

*A slave holding Chamber.*

There are many prominent reminders of Zanzibar's dark history in the slave trade around the island. The market where slaves were confined in dark, airless, underground chambers before being sold still contains the chains bolted to the concrete. A moving memorial now stands where the market once was, reminding visitors of the atrocities committed on that very spot centuries before.

Zanzibar is also well known for the five spices produced there, Vanilla, Black Pepper, Cinnamon, Nutmeg and Ginger and when you walk around the old town you can tell, it smells wonderful.

Dar es Salaam (House of peace in Arabic) was built by Sultan Majid bin Said of Zanzibar in the 1800s but fell into decline after Majid's death in 1870. It was revived in 1887 when the German East Africa Company established a station there. German East Africa was captured by the British during World War I and became Tanganyika. The country gained independence from colonial rule in December 1961 with Dar es Salaam continuing to serve as its capital. In 1964 Tanganyika and Zanzibar merged to form Tanzania.

*Portuguese East Africa*

When I was in both Lourenco Marques and Beira they felt very Portuguese, any beer bought in even the smallest bar came accompanied be a small tray of prawns, nuts and olives and this happened every time you had another beer, it was a lovely place to visit.

*A few beers in Beira and I know what you're thinking but he wasn't!*

# Chapter 8

## Life on the Ocean Wave

By now I had got used to life at sea and although the work was hard all the stewards bonded and worked well together. Going ashore in the various ports was ample compensation for the 15 hours, 7 days a week we were scheduled to be on duty. Working those long days required a sleep in the afternoon on sea days but it was something I never quite got used to and always woke up feeling a bit groggy. Luckily the four of us sharing a cabin employed one of the Lascar seaman as our steward and one of his tasks was to wake us in the afternoon with a cup of tea. He was also responsible for all the laundry and cleaning the cabin, a real God send.

A Lascar sailor was usually from the Indian Subcontinent or Southeast Asia, they had been employed on European ships from the 16th century up until the middle of the 20th century. The word Lashkar is a Persian word derived from the Arabic for guard or soldier and the Portuguese adapted the term to Lascarin meaning seamen. Lascar seamen, always employed as deck hands or in the engine room, were on a three-year contract and very poorly paid so the extra steward work was much sort after. I sadly witnessed the death of one of these hard-working men when in the Indian Ocean. One time during boat drill by the crew the life boat being lowered stuck at one end, throwing this poor fellow onto the side of the ship and into the sea. Of course, the ship made a dramatic turn but by the time another boat could be launched the man had been attacked by sharks and was dead.

One advantage that myself and my fellow stewards had over some other members of the crew was the food we were able to eat. A common practice, although strictly forbidden, was to look at the menu for the passenger's dinner, select what you fancied and order an extra portion to keep in your hot plate. At the end of service, you simply took the plate to the crew mess and enjoyed a first-class meal and of course the menus even back then were exceptional.

*Lascar seamen*

# *Luncheon*

Barley Broth

Suprême of Cod Portugaise

Macaroni Crème au Gratin

Stewed Steak with Tomatoes

Dressed Cabbage
Potatoes : Anna     Baked Jacket

---

### COLD BUFFET

Roast Canterbury Lamb, Mint Sauce
Galantine of Chicken

*Salads :* Lettuce   Beetroot   Onion   Macédoine
*Dressings :* Mayonnaise French Tartare Fines-Herbes

SWEETS
Golden Pudding
Strawberry Ices     Wafer Biscuits

Cheddar Cheese

Dessert                Coffee

*A typical menu of the 60s found in Cabin Saloon
and Tourist Saloon.*

In the sixties of course, there was still a rather rigid class difference and second class was kept very separate from first.

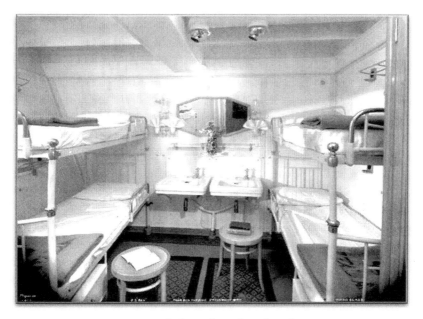

*A second class four berth cabin*

*First class suite*

It's unthinkable now that the difference in cabins was so pronounced.

Ships in the early sixties were used for travelling rather than holiday cruises and the facilities onboard were quite limited. There were few public rooms other than a lounge, restaurant and library/card room. The passengers were very different from today's cruisers, far more formal in their dress, gowns for the ladies, jackets for the men and ties were compulsory with no exceptions. Activities on board were a very limited affair. Shuffleboard, cards the occasional film and if you were lucky, dancing after dinner. There was only one dining room for each class and also one bar. Entertainment consisted of a small orchestra, a pianist, bingo and organised racing using models and dice.

One thing everyone looked forward to when we were at sea was the films shown on deck for the crew. I can vividly remember seeing "Breakfast at Tiffany's" under a jet-black sky with millions of stars and the beautiful Audrey Hepburn on the screen. I must have been feeling a little homesick as the whole scene brought a tear to my eye—big Jessie.

During my time on the Warwick Castle I worked with some real characters and one of my favourites was a very experienced Italian steward by the name of George who would look at the menu and predict what his passengers would want; he then went to get the meals from the galley which he put in his hot plate. George would then persuade his poor passengers that he had selected the best food on the menu and that the other dishes were not up to standard; furthermore, their wait for other items would be seriously long. I don't know how many people insisted on having something not in the hot plate but George was always away before the others and first in the Crew's mess.

*A night off at sea.*

A motley crew – (Second from the left) Rodger from the Savoy, myself and Gwyn Harding.

# Chapter 9

## Table Mountain in all its glory

It wasn't long before the magnificent Table Mountain came into view as we docked in Cape Town, surely one of the best sights in Africa.

Cape Town was one of the places that all the crew wanted time off and I was one of the lucky ones that was able to spend time in this great city. Great bars, the cable car and beaches, shopping on the Parade and much more, Cape Town had it all. We had several South Africans in the crew so the information on where to go was spot on and I was introduced to a drink that rates in my top five beverages, the Brandy square. If my memory serves me correctly it consists of a measure of SA Brandy, one of White Port topped up with ginger ale and served with fresh mint leaves, superb. After all these years I have a hazy memory of the names of the bars we went to but two stick in my mind, The Fireman's Arms and The Perseverance Tavern. I had a holiday in South Africa in the 1990's and it was as great then as in the 60s.

The next two ports of call in SA were East London and Port Elizabeth ending the SA part of the voyage in Durban. Durban was so different to Cape Town, of course in the 60s apartheid was still practised and Cape Town was far more cosmopolitan and relaxed than Durban. Apartheid means "apartness" in Afrikaans and the system that started in 1948 was banned in 1994 when Nelson Mandela became president.

I saw two examples of this dreadful system in action during my time in Durban. The first was on a segregated beach where the white half was equipped with shark nets and barriers and of course the black half of the beach wasn't. It was reported on the day we arrived that yet another black swimmer had been attacked on that beach by a shark and died. The other incident happened when myself and a friend returned by rickshaw to the ship one afternoon. Rickshaws and their pullers have been a part of the Durban scene since the early 1900's, the pullers are mostly Zulus and dress in very elaborate costume. At the dock gates our puller tried to up the price he had originally agreed and was shouting and threatening. A security guard on the dock gates saw this and came over to see what was going on, when he heard what the problem was he started beating the puller with a siambok or leather whip until the guy fled in terror. He told us that they were always trying to get more money out of the tourists and that the display of leaping in the air was not to please the passengers but in an attempt to have loose change roll out of pockets into the back of the seat. I have to say I was shocked to see that a non- official could use violence on someone with complete immunity.

*Durban rickshaw puller*

# Chapter 10

## Where Napoleon trod

Our next two stops were very special, Ascension and St Helena where Napoleon was exiled in October 1815. St Helena was born as a violent volcano in the South Atlantic and is known for its isolation. Jamestown, its capital, became a centre of commerce for the East India Company in the 17th Century.

I can only imagine Napoleon's dismay when he realised he was not being banished to America as he anticipated but to the remote island of St Helena, located 1,200 miles from the nearest landmass off the west coast of Africa. Napoleon's presence could still be felt across the island. The Governor of St Helena's official residence at Plantation House still retains one of Napoleon's chandeliers from Longwood House, his residence while exiled.

Napoleon wasn't the only famous character associated with St Helena, there was Jonathan. Jonathan is a rare Seychelles Giant Tortoise and I had the very special privilege of patting him on the back. It is estimated that Jonathan is between 170 and 200 years old, making him not just St Helena's oldest resident but quite possibly the world's oldest reptile. I believe that Jonathan is now showing his age, he is blind, has lost his sense of smell and now, sadly is alone having lost his companion, Fredric a few years ago, I'm so glad I met him when he was still a sprightly 132 years young.

Until recently the only way to get to St Helena was by sea, which meant a five-night voyage from Cape Town and the only ships sailing that route at the time was the Union Castle Line. From the 19th century St Helena had been served by a Union Castle service that plied between the UK and South Africa, however by the early sixties air travel was steadily taking over from sea travel and Union Castle began to reduce the frequency of its services and in 1977 the route closed. The British Government had to find an alternative way to supplying the Island and they found a ship that could be purchased to fulfil the role. The ship was renamed RMS St Helena and with Princess Margaret on board to launch the service the ship arrived at St Helena on 5th October 1978.

*RMS St Helena*

In 2017, one of humanity's most isolated out-posts joined the twenty-first century and opened what has been described as "the world's most useless airport". With the opening of the airport and the Napoleon connection to the island, the island's legislative council will be hoping for a steady stream of French tourists wanting to see Longwood house.

## Ascension Island

The stop at Ascension was so short that I hardly remember it at all. The Island is a tiny dot of green, a scrap of British territory marooned in the tropical mid-Atlantic halfway between Brazil and Africa. To enter, you must get the written permission of the Queen's representative so there was no shore leave.

The island is named after the day of its discovery, Ascension Day. It was an important safe haven to seafarers and in their day Flying boats. During the second world war it was a naval and air station that provided a base for antisubmarine warfare but it had been a naval garrison from 1815 to 1922. Today the island is a location for the Royal Air Force, a European Space tracking station, an Anglo-American signals facility and a BBC Relay station. The island also plays an important part in the operation of the Global Positional System (GPS).

# Chapter 11

## Long days at sea.

On the way home along the west coast of Africa the stops were few and far between which meant more days at sea. A few entertainments were laid on to keep the crew happy, films, quizzes and dog racing. No, we didn't have six Greyhounds on board, the game was played with life sized wooden dogs and two people rolling dice. The first roll of the dice determined which dog moved and the second roll showed how many feet it went. All this was played out on a large hatch cover and small bets were allowed, it was great fun and a nice night out.

*The Purser and I having a night off at the dogs.*

My time with Union Castle was in the early 60s before the Sexual Offences Act was passed in 1967. It decriminalised homosexual acts in private between two men, both of whom had to have attained the age of 21. The Act applied only to England and Wales and did not cover the Merchant Navy but a lot of gay men had joined the MN before this report came out to avoid criminal prosecution. The Wolfenden committee had been set up to investigate homosexuality and prostitution in 1954. They came to the conclusion that criminal law could not credibly intervene in the private sexual affairs of consenting adults in the privacy of their homes. As a result of this discrimination, every ship I sailed on had its group of gay men, and they enhanced the life of the ship immensely. At no time was I ever bothered by any of my gay shipmates and usually enjoyed their company.

Union Castle required all the stewards to buy their own spare white steward's jacket and as these got grubby quite quickly you needed a minimum of three. A fellow steward, a Maltese guy called Max said he had a couple spare and I could buy one.

The deal was done and I assumed that payment could wait until we were paid off at the end of the cruise but after a few days another Maltese fellow came to see me and told me of Max's criminal record for violence, the money was with Max that very night!

Being a steward had another advantage over other members of the crew - olive oil and vinegar. This was in the days before sun cream was readily available and olive oil seemed to be a cheap alterative. The stewards had of course access to both in the dining room and some became dealers! I have no idea why we mixed the oil with vinegar and hate to think the damage done to our skin but I do remember being a nice shade of brown most of the time.

*I rest my case! That's me in the uniform cap*

# Chapter 12

## The Last Leg

Two ports to go and I was beginning to think about getting home and in my opinion, some well-earned leave.

Madeira first and what a lovely little island it is. Funchal the capital is backed by hills and known for its harbour, gardens and Madeira wine, which I sampled extensively in some of the many cellars around the city.

Funchal's history goes back over 5 centuries, when early Portuguese settlers colonised the coast of the bay where fennel (funcho) grew in abundance, giving its name to the new town of Funchal. The cobbled streets in the centre with their cafes, bars and wine cellars make Funchal an interesting city. The one thing everyone stopping off at Madeira wants to do is the toboggan ride. This terrifying ride starts in Monte and finishes in Livramento some 1.5 miles below.

Originally a fast means of transport down to Funchal for people living in Monte, the toboggan appeared around 1850 and are two-seater wicker sledges that glide on wooden runners, pushed and steered by two men traditionally dressed in white cotton clothes and a straw hat, using their rubber-soled boots as brakes. The journey takes about 10 minutes reaching at times a speed of 48 km/hour. I did it then but never again.

Madeira is also known for its flowers and I could not resist buying some to take back to my mother. I bought an absolutely huge bunch of orchids which I managed to store in the now almost empty cold store and a week later they were still looking great.

Las Palmas the last port of call and the last place for a few drinks with some of the fellows I had been working with for all those weeks. It transpired that a bar called "Casanova's" was the place to go and myself and three friends set out to sample some of this Madeira wine.

*Myself and Gwyn Harding at the other end*

The most charismatic man I had ever met at that time was one Gwyn Harding, a Welshman from Llandudno. A former civil servant with the Ministry of Agriculture, he was the ship's Doctor's Steward and a man full of schemes on how to get rich quick. Another prolific drinker who also liked a wager, and one such wager was that he would drink a full pint of anything put in a pint glass, I would not have believed this had I not seen it with my own eyes. The rules of the bet were that he should down the pint in one go but with no time imposed and not be sick for at least one hour afterwards. I can't tell you the full contents of that pint; suffice it to say there were at least five different spirits and a small amount of Guinness to make him bring the whole lot up. Word had spread around the ship and a lot of cash was being waged; Gwyn took on a large proportion of the bets himself and didn't seem to acknowledge that this could kill him. The corridor outside his cabin was packed with every one thinking they would be a bit richer by that evening. The concoction was mixed, and Gwyn stood up to drink. Very slowly the potent mix disappeared down Gwyn's throat until the glass was empty. Gwyn looked a bit dazed and staggered to the heads, wobbled about a bit in front of one, and raised the hopes of the assembled spectators. But he wasn't sick and after five minutes or so staggered back to his cabin and to the sound of groans from the onlookers, promptly passed out on his bunk. Gwyn was missing from his duties the next day but won over £100 that afternoon however, I'm sure unimaginable damage to his health was done. One of Gwyn's get-rich-quick schemes was to try and bring ashore in the UK a large quantity of cigarettes to resell at a profit. Given that cigarettes at crew prices in the Sixties were very low, the scheme was feasible but of course highly illegal. Gwyn's idea was to pack a large suitcase with cigarettes and include it in the ship doctor's baggage, and as it was he who carried the bags ashore, he felt that no customs officer would search a doctor's case. How wrong he was, as the doc was stopped but of course denied the that suitcase was his. Gwyn stated that it was outside the doctor's cabin so he naturally thought it was to be taken landside. The cigarettes were confiscated but no one was fined. I remained friends with Gwyn after we both left the Navy. The crew price of cigarettes at the time was nine old shillings for two hundred but the duty was raised and they went up to eleven shillings. I said that I'm not paying that price and promptly gave up this unhealthy habit for the rest of my life.

Returning back to Britain through the Bay of Biscay, a force nine gale blew up, galleys were closed, and the passengers were told to remain in their cabins. We lost a lot of crockery and there were a lot of very seasick people on board, including me. I managed to last a day or so but then took to my bunk, not caring if the ship went down or not, until we reached the English Channel. My fellow cabin mates said that they have never quite seen such deep shades of green on someone's face before, but if you have ever been really seasick you will know how I felt. The Warwick Castle was a very small ship by today's standards, being only 17,400 tons against the modern liners of 100,000 tons plus, and she could roll alarmingly in a heavy swell.

The final of any voyage of course ended when the ship entered the English Channel and the crew were very prone to something we called "channel fever", a sense of euphoria and a tendency to celebrate the home coming a little too much. The evening before we docked was, for the stewards, "Tip Time" and if one had had a full complement of passengers you could quite easily accumulate as much as your wages, which were payed at the end of the trip. This was also reckoning time where you paid your own steward, and mess bill and the Seamans Union who were always there to collect your dues.

The ship was cleared and it wasn't long before I was in a taxi heading home. When my mother saw me, she burst into tears over how I looked. I had gone from a generous 10.5 stone to a very slim 9 stone but her wonderful cooking soon got me back to my fighting weight.

After each voyage, three of us, Gwyn Harding, Rodger from the Savoy, and myself, always arranged to meet up on the first night of our leave, and the venue was always the same, dog racing at the White City Stadium and off to the Aberdeen Steakhouse in Leicester Square for a good late supper. I was never a great gambler and never lost much money, however I must have inherited a love of racing from my dear old dad because I did like a night out at the dogs. Gwyn and I enjoyed the buzz of the White City and the odd small flutter but Rodger was a serious punter. On one night, we had to pay for his meal because he had a run of bad luck and gambled away the whole of his pay from a two-month voyage. We never saw Rodger again after that night. I presume he went back to sea earlier than he needed to earn more betting money. The White City Stadium was built in the White City area of London for the 1908 Summer Olympics. It hosted swimming, speedway, and a match in the 1966 World Cup. From 1927 until 1984 it was the premier venue for greyhound racing, hosting the English Greyhound Derby. The stadium was demolished in 1985.

*White City Stadium*

I did two trips on the Warwick Castle at the end of which I thought it was time to see another bit of the world and so I joined P & O.

# Chapter 13

## The Guards of the Sea

A couple of weeks after I left the Warwick Castle I was once again at the "Seamans Employment Exchange" signing on another ship and this time it was with P & O.

In those days, different shipping lines had set areas of the world in which they operated with their ships, carrying people to a particular destination rather than just cruising. Joining P&O in the Sixties was a big step up as the crew of P&O ships considered themselves to be the "guards of the sea". The move gave me a whole new part of the world to explore and on 8 January 1962 I joined the SS Iberia at Tilbury Docks for a four-month voyage to New Zealand. Originally a constituent of the Peninsular and Oriental Steam Navigation Company, P&O is the oldest cruise line in the world, having operated the world's first passenger ships in the early nineteenth century.

The Iberia was first registered in 1954 and taken out of service in 1972. She had a gross tonnage of 29.614 tons and was built by Harland & Wolff in Belfast and carried a crew of 700+.

On joining the Iberia, I had been promoted to the first-class dining saloon and shared a cabin with only two other people rather than the three on the Warwick Castle. Although I was nineteen years old, this was a different time from today; I was still somewhat naive in the ways of the world. On being shown my cabin, I couldn't help noticing that of the three bunks, two were covered in the normal P&O bedding but one was decked out in a red silk bedspread and matching curtains. When I asked, "Why the difference?" I was told, "Oh, that's Rachael's bunk!"

Such was my naivety at the time, I genuinely thought, "great, mixed cabins!", but of course they weren't. Rachael turned out to be 6 feet 3 inches, built like a brick outhouse with an awful yellow dye job and the campest manner I had ever at the time seen. Rachael looked after his two much younger cabin mates like a mother hen and was always on hand to offer advice on where to go and which bars to visit, although some of his choices were best avoided! On one occasion, going ashore in Naples, myself and two friends were making our way out of the dock gates when we spotted Rachael coming the other way in some state. He was bleeding from the mouth and his clothes were torn. Very concerned, we rushed up to him and asked what had happened. He said, "I've been attacked, dear."

Three thugs had set about him in one of Naples less salubrious areas but luckily hadn't managed to relieve him of his money or Seaman's book. We helped him back to the ship and made sure he was okay before continuing our night out. One of these friends, a great guy called Theo, was Swiss and as such could speak and read Italian and was in the habit of getting a local newspaper when he could get his hands on one. This was such a day and he could hardly contain his excitement to tell us of a story that appeared in that mornings edition of *Corriere di Napoli*. It appeared that the police were looking for a large tall blond man who was flamboyantly dressed and had beaten three young Italian men, putting one in hospital. We certainly couldn't think who that man may have been, but speculation came to an end that evening when the ship sailed!

Life on the Iberia was far more civilised than with Union Castle. For one thing, I didn't have to load stores or clean decks and the crew accommodation was much better and although still classed as a hanging offence, we always chose from the first-class passenger menu for our late dinner. During my time with P&O I experienced some great meals which gave me a lifelong appreciation of fine food.

My Swiss friend Theo and I usually worked the same duties and had the same free time so we normally went ashore together. One run ashore that sticks in my mind was Athens where we hired a scooter and toured the sights. The sight of the Parthenon as we rode up towards it was one I shall never forget. It was the first such structure I had ever seen and to my mind is still the most impressive. The Parthenon is a former temple dedicated to the goddess Athena, whom the people of Athens considered their patron. It is the most important surviving building of classical Greece and one of the world's greatest cultural monuments. Unfortunately, on our way back to the ship, the scooter broke down, but with the help of a friendly amateur mechanic we were soon speeding back and arrived in time for the dinner service.

*SS Iberia*

*Theo and me on our way to the Parthenon*

## The dreaded nursery duty

One duty to strike fear into all the stewards on the Iberia was to see your name posted on the order board for nursery duty. This involved organising and helping out at children's mealtimes in the nursery. The little darlings usually had their mothers in attendance so prohibited you from using physical violence. One of my colleagues found a novel way to get around this, he wrapped a large serving spoon in a napkin and when a child was being very naughty he would give them a little flick with the napkin while making soothing noises, it seemed to work and as far as I know he was never prosecuted for child abuse. Bear in mind this was the sixties and caning in schools was still permitted.

*The nursery- still gives me nightmares*

Another duty we were tasked with but, unlike the nursery stint, this one was much sought after - the ice cream or beef tea duty. The deck hands would set up a table on deck and the steward would bring up from the galley an urn of hot beef tea in the cold weather or cartons of ice cream in the hot weather. The popularity of this duty had many advantages, it got you off serving lunch, it was nice to be working outside, it was a very easy task and the main reason on warm days was you could check out the girls in their swim suits.

*The tourist dining room where I started to appreciate good food and to dislike bad mannered passengers.*

*The Tourist smoking room*

# Chapter 14

## The Cruise of a Lifetime

P & O ships embarked from Tilbury or Southampton and on this occasion, it was at Tilbury that I joined the ship for my longest cruise. The Iberia departed on 1st January 1962 and returned on 28th April and I was working in the first-class dining saloon for the first time. Memory dims with age so you will forgive me if I chronical the stops out of sync somewhat. A place I went to on two trips was Bombay, now Mumbai and I can still see the colour, hear the noise and remember the throngs of people. I remember I bought a large leather!! trunk which during the voyage acquired loads of luggage stickers.

I kept this trunk for many years after I left the navy but the paper-thin leather coating started to peel after about three weeks, still it looked pretty cool carrying it up the road going home.

I think Singapore was probably the next port and with a smart shirt on it was off to Raffles Hotel for a legendary Singapore Sling. This cocktail has always been synonymous with Raffles Hotel, made basically of Gin, cherry brandy and Benedictine. I think it possibly cost us a day's pay but it was worth it to experience one in this wonderful setting.

A few weeks into the voyage and Suva the capital of Fiji came around and with it one of the strangest experiences I ever had, it was called Kava. It's a popular drink with the locals and sometimes called, Yaona. It's made from the root of a pepper plant and its effects include a numbing of the tongue and lips, relaxed muscles and it tastes awful, like muddy water. It also has the effect of putting you to sleep but in the morning the headache you're left with is appalling.

During our stay in Suva a Rugby match was arranged with the local police. Well we had some burly guys among the deck hands and were pretty confident, that is until we saw their team. I think the Fiji police have a height requirement and its 6 feet 8 inches; also, you must weigh over 18 stone. I thank my lucky stars that I was just a supporter, needless to say we lost very badly.

# Chapter 15

## Life in First Class

P & O and working in the first-class saloon was a great step up from Union Castle and life was considerably better, although still required to work long hours 7 days a week you tended to get more time off. Still required to hump cases of wine etc up to the bars and restaurants but this was carried out at about 7.00am and not 6.00am.

For a short time during this trip I was asked to fill in as a wine waiter in the second-class dining room and for that period life got even more relaxed. I was given a short lesson on the wines available in second class and was thrown in at the deep end. Luckily, I was fortunate to have a very decent and knowledgeable head waiter who I always relied on to advise me when needed. I think I did reasonably well but remember one rather obnoxious passenger who ordered a bottle of champagne, the cheapest, and when I brought the glasses (saucer type that were used onboard at the time) he blew his top and ranted and insisted on having flute glasses, called me liar when I told him that those glasses were not available onboard and only calmed down when the assistant head waiter verified my claim. He told me later that they did have flutes in First Class but he wasn't going to send someone for them for "that jumped up so and so".

In the 1st class dining saloon P&O produced some beautiful printed covers for their menus and I had the foresight to save a small collection depicting ships and boats from the various countries the SS Iberia passed through. In pastel water colours and some illustrated by David Knight they feature Caiques in the Eastern Mediterranean, Dhows in the Arabian Sea and my absolute favourite, Sailing Barges in the river Thames.

*A selection of P & O menu covers from the 60s*

Union Castle had only one uniform for all weathers but P & O had a tropical one, white jackets, trousers, and shoes. Their method of ordering a change from one to "whites" was just to put a standing order on the crew notice board. One morning I reported for the breakfast service without looking at the standing orders and yes, at 8.00am I still had cold weather uniform on. Again, the kind assistant head waiter came to my aid by chatting to my passengers while I managed to change avoiding a dressing down by the chief steward.

*The assistant head waiter, my saviour I when I did a stint as a wine waiter.*

I remember that I had to hold onto the chair, and it wasn't because of the ship's motion, it was a tough life as a wine waiter.

# Chapter 16

## The Tailor of Hong Kong

While in Singapore, both passengers and crew had the opportunity of ordering and having handmade shirts and suits made. Tailors from Hong Kong would join the ship and advertise their services, you would be measured up for your shirt or suit and they would radio the measurements through to their workshops in Hong Kong. When the ship arrived in Hong Kong a few days later the goods would be ready for a first fitting.

In those far distant days I was quite a snappy dresser with both handmade shirts as well as suits. I think the tailor I used was a Mr Nathan but only because his shop was in Nathan Road, and he and an assistant came aboard to take the orders. It was obviously worth his while to pay for his passage back to Hong Kong and measure up anyone wanting a suit or shirt. When you docked in Hong Kong, Mr Nathan's staff would be waiting for your first fitting and the next day your beautifully fitted suit would be delivered to the ship. I think I had two suits and a blazer and a few shirts made, the suits in a silk mohair Mod style and the shirts with cutaway collars and monogrammed on the front. I must have thought I looked a million dollars as all my old school friends were still wearing Burton suits that looked like they were made for other people—unkind but true. I have since had shirts made while on holiday in Bangkok but they never came up to the quality and style of Mr Nathan.

One of the best boat rides in the world was on a green and white Star Ferry on the route between Hong Kong Island and Kowloon. The history of Star Ferry's goes back to 1888 when the Kowloon Ferry company was founded by one Dorabjee Mithaiwala. Ten years later it was bought by a British businessman, Sir C P Chater and the name was changed to the Star Ferry Company. All the names of the ferries were inspired by Alfred Lord Tennyson's epic poem, "Crossing the Bar" and comes from the line "Sunset and evening star, and one clear call for me". In its hundred years+ beginning it has gone from four single deck coal powered boats to a fleet of twelve diesel electric vessels that hold up to 700 passengers on two decks in air-conditioned comfort.

Today the ferries depart every 20 minutes and carry over 50,000 passengers every day, an important service in the Hong Kong transport system.

*One of the distinctive green and white Star Ferries*

So, Hong Kong, all suited and booted we hit this impressive city. I had been looking forward to this for some time and wanted to start the night with some real Chinese food, big mistake if you try to go for authenticity.

After a few drinks we came across a small very local restaurant and in the interest of sampling the "real food of Hong Kong", we went in. Of course, the small board on the wall acting as the menu was in Cantonese, so it was down to just pointing to an item and hoping for the best and best is not a word I would use for the two dishes they produced. One dish was some part of a chicken but I couldn't say which part because it was covered in a strong vinegar like brown sauce and the second offering was a large bowl of something very fishy, I know it was a fish dish because the heads were still floating on top. Any semblance of hunger instantly vanished and we left for, perhaps, a not so local restaurant. We went from the ridiculous to the sublime in Aberdeen Harbour - The Tai Pak Floating Restaurant where we had a great meal.

*The Tai Pak Floating Restaurant*

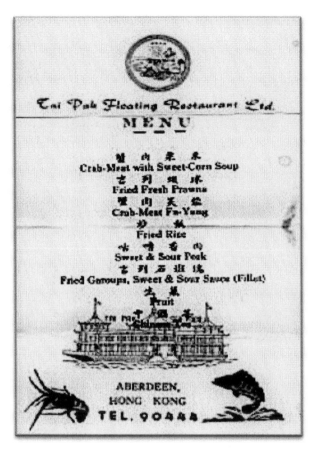

*The Tai Pak Floating Restaurant menu*

During our four-day stopover in HK, for a lot of our passengers this was their final destination and so the ship was only half occupied, which meant that the crew got more time off. Myself and two friends decided that we should see a bit more of the country and so one afternoon took off for the New Territories for an overnight stay. We stayed in a small hotel called the Red House and were told that the distant mountains were in Communist China, a sight, along with the Star Ferries going over to Kowloon, that I will never forget. I wish I still had those suits though.

# Chapter 17

## Crossing the Line

During this voyage we had crossed the Equator and this involved the dreaded "Crossing the Line" ceremony for both passengers and crew alike. Naval tradition dictates that any ship crossing the equator must pay their respects to the Lord of the Seas, King Neptune to gain his acceptance. Everybody on board the ship must be presented to Neptune's Court during the infamous Ceremony and the ritual requires all those who had never previously crossed the line to be charged for their crimes and get the justice they deserve. King Neptune is said to be the ruler of the seas and this entire shindig is orchestrated to appease the King by showing him respect and to keep all on the ship from the perils of the sea and to bring good luck. One of the crew is made to dress up as King Neptune, with the Trident sceptre in hand and a crown on his head, beside him is seated his wife, Queen Amphitrite and they're both joined by Davy Jones and members of his court for this royal procedure.

The tradition of crossing the line began with the Navy over 400 years ago and given its long history, the ritual has changed over the years but it remains a well-known, albeit sometimes controversial, part of Naval culture and commercial cruise lines ritual. Though ceremonies differ, there's a general form and a common cast of characters. King Neptune is a prominent figure, as is his representative Davy Jones. Other people often show up, including a surgeon, a barber, people dressed as bears, and a judge. These roles are all played by "shellbacks" those who have gone through the ritual before with the first-time participants known as "pollywogs".

*King Neptune & Co.*

After the ritual everyone gets a certificate to show they have crossed the line and are safe from further abuse.

The ceremonies that I have witnessed involving cruise passengers are far different than those that the crew suffer and suffer is the word. The passengers are covered with things like flour, jam and soap suds whereas with the crew the items used are used oil, fish water (from the galley) treacle, eggs (preferably rotten) and other items of a disgusting nature. The equator virgins are hunted down and covered from head to tail with the aforementioned mixture and this isn't done in a gentle manner! Whereas the passengers have the pool to clean off in, (it is emptied and refilled after) the crew only have a hose pipe on the heads. I recall that it took ages to get the stuff out of my hair and I'm sure that at the evening dinner that night I was several shades darker than before and the smell was with me for days. Sadly, I never crossed the line again and therefore never had the pleasure of seeing other first timers suffer.

# Chapter 18

## Australia

Australia beckoned and I had four ports to look forward to, Perth, Adelaide, Melbourne and Sydney. The first two were only quick turnarounds so although I did step ashore in both I don't recall much about them. However, I thought Melbourne a great city. One of the oldest pubs in an area called Prahran is The Windsor Castle Hotel and although a tram- ride out of the centre it was one of the places to make for and having that name made me feel right at home.

*The original hotel was built in 1871 and the rebuilt Windsor Castle is a typical Victorian pub.*

I stopped in Melbourne a few years ago and was astounded by the change in the place. Melbourne of the 60s had no high-rise buildings however now would rival New York but still a great place to visit.

*Sydney*

There are, in my opinion, only so many truly impressive places in the world to arrive by sea and Sydney is one of them. The Harbour Bridge is very impressive, the Opera house not fully open until 1973. The bridge, which was opened in 1932, is the largest steel arch span in the world being 1149 meters long. It weighs 52,800 tons and most of the steel was imported from the UK, it took eight years to build and cost $4.2 and I docked just underneath.

*The Iberia in Sydney harbour*

Australians are known for their beer drinking; so, when we arrived and went ashore we felt morally bound to keep the reputation of the Merchant Navy at its highest and that involved sinking a few tinnies. Where is the best place to head for to achieve this? the Rocks area and that's where one of Australia's oldest hotel is - The Fortune of War. After that head for The Hero of Waterloo and finish at The Lord Nelson Brewery Hotel, a good night out. The Lord Nelson was originally a private home built in 1836 from sandstone blocks quarried by convicts from the base of Observatory Hill. A liquor licence was granted in 1842 and the hotel opened its doors which have remained open ever since. The Rocks is a neighbourhood of small lanes and has some of Sydney's oldest pubs and in the 60s was a bit wild, to put it mildly. I remember being told of a legend who was the barmaid in a pub in George Street, The Royal George. Naturally myself and a few friends, who had never seen a legend, headed for the Royal George and sure enough there she was standing behind a huge long bar in all her glory. The biggest "Norks" (Australian slang) that this young lad had ever seen and only half covered, the beer was good too. The other area in Sydney that was not for the retiring type was Kings Cross, although I was warned that not all the "ladies" one may come across on the Forbes Street steps were what they seemed!

It wasn't only public houses we went to, in fact I spent a lovely day on the famous Bondi Beach. Deadly warnings circulating amongst the crew about the number of fatal shark attacks at the beach kept me well out of the water but the sand and sun were splendid. There are shark nets but that didn't stop some 7/8 attacks a year and I am very attached to all my limbs.

After this visit I didn't see Sydney for forty years and when I did the sight leaving the harbour with the Sydney Opera house on one side and the bridge on the other was even more spectacular, one of life's great views.

# Chapter 19

## New Zealand or is it Scotland?

My first sight of New Zealand came very early one morning in February 1962 and I thought that I had been in a coma for three weeks and the ship was just steaming past the Scottish Highlands. It was misty, raining and cold but I must say still looked spectacular. Later the next day we arrived in Auckland and I thought it was one of the nicest cities to visit.

As crew we used our British Seaman's card (our form of passport) to go ashore but this entailed waiting until the Immigration Authorities had cleared all the passengers. The Immigration Officers came aboard and set up an embarkation desk for the passengers to present their passports and we were told when we were allowed to leave the ship. This happened in several countries including the USA and parts of the Caribbean. However, those savvy members of the crew and believe it or not; I was in that group, had their own passports and were able to present them to the Authorities and get clearance early. I duly asked the Officer for a stamp in my passport, he knew I was crew and I made a joke about collecting endorsements. Luckily, he took it in a light-hearted manner and stamped not one but two endorsements and I happily made my way to the gangway. It wasn't until later that I looked at the stamps and discovered what he had stamped in the passport. He had a greater sense of humour than I credited him with because one of the endorsement he gave me probably made me one of the only persons in the world to be asked to comply with his instruction It was; -

AGRICULTURE INSPECTION REQUIRED

*The endorsement can be seen on page 7*
*but I never did go to see the Vet.*

Ironically a few years after I left the Merchant Navy I became one of Her Majesty's Immigration Officers and always like to think that I remembered this incident and tried to keep a sense of humour in a very demanding job.

Going ashore in New Zealand for a drink in the 60s wasn't as easy as one would think, the pubs closed at six o clock every night and this became known as "The six-o clock Swill". This was introduced as a temporary wartime measure in 1917 and was not repealed until a national referendum was held in 1967 when 64 % of voters supported a move to 10.00pm closing. If by some miracle you could get to a pub before 6.00 pm the place to go was the Shakespeare Hotel but sadly I never made it and had to spend my free time in Auckland in cafes and coffee shops.

# Chapter 20

## Manila

Manila in the sixties was considered to be one of the most dangerous places on the planet, so much so that we were all given lectures on what to avoid and stern warnings that under no circumstances should we go ashore at night by ourselves. As a consequence of this I didn't see much of the city but as with all the ports of call there was always some "old salt" who knew what to do and where to go and in Manila it was definitely a cock fight. In those days I was always looking for new experiences, it seems rather bizarre now why I would have wanted to see to chickens tearing each other to pieces but never the less three of us decided to try to find a fight.

The Philippines is one of the few countries in the world to legalise cockfighting, the fights are usually held on Sundays. The cocks or roosters are pitted against each other and fight with steel spurs strapped to their legs. The birds are naturally aggressive towards each other and fight until one is dead or is unable to continue. To Filipinos cockfighting is more than just entertainment, the arenas are packed with men and probably 99% of them gamble on the outcome of each fight.

So, the three of us piled into a taxi at the dock gates and tried to tell the driver what we wanted to do, this had its problems due to the language differences but we set off and after a surprisingly short time we arrived at a very dilapidated house. With encouragement from our driver we knocked on the door and to our amazement found ourselves not at a cockfighting arena but a brothel. The taxi driver, who was still parked outside, had obviously picked up three sailors and what do sailors want on a night out but some female company. We quickly made our exit from this house of sin and again tried to explain that it wasn't the two-legged birds we craved but the feathered variety. Again, we set off and arrived at a more imposing house, you guessed it, it was a more expensive brothel. At this point we had rather gone off the idea of cockfighting and told (gestured) the driver to take us back to a bar just outside the docks. I think in hindsight that we were probably secretly relieved not to have found a cockfight that night.

Cockfighting in Manila

# Chapter 21

## Shore Leave in the Swinging Sixties

Being away for the best part of the first two years of the sixties I missed a lot of what was happening with London and my friends. Of course, I had leave while back in the UK but never really connected with the swinging sixties until I left the Merchant Navy. When out with some of my friends from school we seemed to have nothing in common any more, I still had a girlfriend but the long separations paid the toll and we split up just after I left the Navy.

Friends would talk about groups, singers and records that I had never heard of and while I was free to come and go they all had jobs. Another bone of contention was money, I was well paid; lived rent free and also had my gratuities to spend whereas they had rather limited resources. This put a damper on the places we could go and the times we went out.

That didn't stop us painting the town on Saturday night. The choice meeting place depended on whether we met in Chelsea and went on to Soho or Earls Court and stayed locally. Chelsea pubs were The Chelsea Potter on the King's Road or the Anglesey Arms and if it was Earls Court it was the King's Head or the Bolton.

The King's Head was somewhat notorious in the sixties due to one Christine Keeler who was a patron of the pub, sadly I can't claim to have seen her during my visits. It was said that Miss Keeler used to drink there before she moved on to the wild parties of the 60s. If we met up in Soho the meeting place was Bar Italia in Frith Street, the best coffee house in London. This wonderful café was opened in 1949 and is open 20 hours a day and I still go there for my coffee when I'm in Soho. After a coffee we usually went on to the French Pub or the French House as it's known to it patrons. After a few beers we moved on to a jazz club, The Marquee in Oxford Street or Studio 51 better known as the Ken Collier Club.

A member of the crew that I had been quite friendly with was David from the Pursers Office, we discovered that he had a flat just off the Portobello Road, some half a mile from where my parents lived. David was a bit older than me and like me loved the clubs and pubs of Soho, he was even a member of the famous drinking club, the Colony Club in Dean Street. This great club was of course open when the pubs were closed and David kindly took me there as a guest.

The membership list reads like a Who's Who of the entertainment industry and in the sixties included, the artist Francis Bacon. George Melly and Lucian Freud. David Bowie and even Princess Margaret were among the guests to have visited the club, again I didn't see any of them but was thrilled one afternoon to see a hero of mine, Long John Baldry, one of the best voices of the 60s and who was responsible for helping such artists as Elton John and Rod Stewart.

I still had a Lambretta scooter in those days so it was easy for me to get about London, which of course wasn't the traffic clogged place it is today. You were able to park on a lot of roads in central London even with a car and a scooter parked outside Bar Italia, where a scooter club met up, was perfectly safe overnight. Happy days.

# Chapter 22

## Japan, not what I expected

*Kobe*

My first glimpse of Japan was the city of Kobe and it was not what I expected, it looked like any other big city. Kobe is located on the Island of Honshu, has a nice harbour and mountain and today is known for its Kobe beef.

However, mountains and beef weren't the first things on my mind when I stepped ashore that first night and armed with the names of several bars (Navy grapevine) we ventured in to the city. The bars we sought were in the older part of town and my first impression was "why is it so dark" - street lighting seemed not to have reached Japan in the sixties. The bars were so different from anything I had experienced before, customer service unequalled.

Two of the many bars of choice were the Bar V and the Hit Bar and as you can see from these old bar cards almost everything was available. Kobe was the only place in the world that I have been totally lost, with not a single sign in English and no one having the slightest idea of what I was saying, it was like being on another planet. Late one night trying to get back to the ship I stopped a taxi but the only way I could tell him where I wanted to go was with elaborate gestures and signs. He eventually seemed to gather that I was a sailor and we set off, mercifully my hand gestures of the sea and waves got me back to the dock gates.

*Street of bars and noodle cafes in Yokohama*

## *Yokohama*

Yokohama is the second largest city after Tokyo but the old city was destroyed in 1923 by a huge earthquake. It was rebuilt but again destroyed by the US air force during World War 11 so most of what was around in 1960s dated from the 50s.

As the ship was in Yokohama for a few of days I took some time off and myself and a friend took the train to Tokyo. This was in the days before the bullet trains, which I believe now take about 15 minutes but this took over an hour before we were in the middle of Tokyo and the Ginza. The Ginza (silver mint) is Tokyo's famous shopping, dining and entertainment district. Dominating the area is the Ginza Wako building its clock tower, built in 1932, is the symbol of the Ginza. After lunch in a noddle bar and a walk around we sadly had to catch the train back to Yokohama but the brief visit was one I will never forget.

Before returning to the ship that afternoon I wanted to do a bit of shopping for a present for my Mother. I found a small department store and was bowed in at the door by two young ladies in uniform. The service was like nothing I had ever come across, one was treated as if you were the store owner. I bought a tea set, highly decorated with the face of a geisha in the bottom of each cup, pretty fancy stuff for the 60s. Again, on departing the store the doors were held open and more bows executed, a great shopping experience.

I still had the night off and once again went into town and found a rather ordinary bar but with the most extraordinary barmaid and I was completely smitten. The bar was the San Francisco and even after all these years I still remember this gorgeous geisha's name, Junko Tanaka. We seemed to hit it off and I know she was there to serve drinks and encourage customers to buy more but I never felt that this was why she talked to me for most of the night. Unusually for the 60s, she did speak a little English and when the bar closed at about 1.00am Junko suggested that myself and my friend join her and another girl from the bar for a late bite to eat.

*Reddish Brown Japanese Dragon Tea Set*

I was so taken with this lovely Japanese girl that I arranged to see her at the bar the next day; I was absent for duty for this and as a consequence was Logged. This is where you are up before the Captain and disciplinary action is taken, this action is noted in the official log book of the voyage, I was fined a day's pay. I remember taking Junko a pack of 200 cigarettes as they were very expensive in Japan but very cheap on board. Alas this was to be our last meeting as the ship sailed that night, some of my crew mates said that it was quite common for crew to jump ship in Japan over bar girls but thankfully I had a little more common sense but never the less, left with a heavy heart after my "Madam Butterfly" episode.

I think I picked the right bar to go to that night, most of my fellow stewards chose one called *Sakaba* and the tales they told cannot be repeated here, I will just show the bar card for the establishment and leave it to one's imagination!

Japan was the most different place I have even been to and when I see some of the Japanese TV shows today I can see that nothing has changed, they are extremely pleasant but so different from us in the west as to be from another planet, still I did enjoy my Japanese adventure.

# Chapter 23

## Canada

The next stop on the cruise was Vancouver and our arrival in this great Canadian city was truly memorable. While coming into the pier the Iberia apparently was going a trifle too fast and hit the wooden dock. No damage to the ship but it demolished some six feet of wooden pier.

Vancouver in the winter months was covered in snow and very cold and not very enticing for a trip ashore and it seemed that the old salt's knowledge on where to go in Vancouver was somewhat lacking, some said that it was all flower power and coffee bars and that the few bars around the dock area were dingy old places.

The people of Vancouver called their city, The City of Love and Revolution and I think it was the first time I had encountered the "Hippie" lifestyle. On my one brief trip ashore, dressed in non-winter clothes, it did seem that there were a large number of young Vancouverites displaying a lot of facial hair and colourful strange clothes. Although I was just above the legal drinking age of 19 in Canada; it was agreed that we would find a café and go for a coffee and a bite to eat instead of a few pints. After a stroll in the freezing cold we settled on the first warm looking place we came across, the comforting sounding "Ovaltine Café" on East Hastings Street.

I later found that the Ovaltine Café was an institution in Vancouver, opened in 1942, the year that I was born, it hadn't changed much from its neon sign to the classic interior. With red vinyl stools running along a long bar and high wooden booths it was a real find but not a patch on Bar Italia in Soho.

# Chapter 24

## The United States of America

One port I will always remember was San Francisco, mainly for four reasons. One, I bought my first real pair of jeans direct from the Levi shop where they were made. In keeping with the trendy practice of the day, I got a pair one size too big. Now, at home you got into your jeans, filled up the bath, sat in it, and hoped they moulded to your shape, but in the crew quarters this wasn't an option and so one tied them to a length of strong rope and dangled them out of the porthole into the sea overnight. This not only shrunk them but gave a nice faded look. It's not known how many pairs of jeans were lost at sea but they certainly looked the business on runs ashore.

Levi Strauss & Co was founded in 1853 and was the inventor of jeans. The pre-shrunk version didn't come out until 1962 hence having to buy one size too big and shrink them yourself.

The second reason I remember the port was that I was thrown off a San Francisco tram; well, asked to get off, and all because I was eating a hot dog while travelling.

*This is the very same store on Market Street where I bought
my jeans and it doesn't look any different from 1962.*

And the third memorable event occurred when a group of
us went out one night to a bar/nightclub, the Longbar
Showboat Club. As I was the only one in the party under
twenty-one, I was not allowed in the main bar and had to
spend the night in a rather dark and cold side room on my
own without a clear view of the stage and drinking Coca Cola
all night. Believe I missed Ella Fitzgerald, and I have hated
Coca Cola ever since. Ella Fitzgerald performed in San
Francisco during every decade from 1930 to the 80s, she was
resident at the Longbar where she performed to packed
crowds.

There was a lot of talk of another bar that was one of the best for Jazz, The Saloon. Operating since 1861 and still going but I was told it was quite small and didn't have an underage room so there was no point in seeking it out.

However, the thing that sticks in my mind on that port of call was the sight of Alcatraz. Alcatraz Island is located in San Francisco Bay, 1.25 miles offshore from the main land. The island was developed as a lighthouse, military prison (1828) and from 1934 until 1963 a federal prison. Alcatraz was designed to hold prisoners classed as too troublesome to be incarcerated in other prisons. On 11th August 1934 the first batch of prisoners arrived in handcuffs escorted by 60 FBI and US Marshals, most of the first inmates were notorious bank robbers or murders. During its 29 years as a prison it held some of America's most famous criminals including Al Capone and Robert Stroud, the birdman of Alcatraz. A total of 36 prisoners made 14 escape attempts, 23 were caught, six were shot dead, 2 drowned, and 5 were listed as missing presumed drowned, the prison authorities claimed that no prisoner had successfully escaped.

In 1962 when the Iberia passed by Alcatraz it was still a fully operating prison and on this particular morning the island looked dark and foreboding in the rain and a slight mist. We passed quite close and as I watched it slide by I can remember thinking that the very sight of the place alone would have kept me on the straight and narrow for life.

*Alcatraz State Penitentiary*

# Chapter 25

## Istanbul- the first visit of many.

I feel that like Venice everyone should visit Istanbul at least once in their life time, it is so very different than other cities and to sail down the Bosphorus and see the city from the water is truly unforgettable. Historically known as Constantinople it straddles the Bosphorus Straits which separates Europe and Asia. Not having a lot of time ashore I don't think I visited any of the magnificent sights the city has to offer but several of us ended up late at night in a large café overlooking the city. We started talking to a father and his daughter and got on so well he ordered us a Hookah also known as a Galyan. This is an instrument for vaporizing and smoking flavoured tobacco, the smoke is passed through water in the base before inhaling. Of course, we had to partake but I can't say the experience was enjoyable. I got talking to the daughter who was about my age and was completely smitten, we even exchanged addresses but alas I never followed it up and never heard from this dark eyed beauty again.

To experience a glorious sight and Istanbul at its best you should walk across the Galata Bridge at sunset. The city is silhouetted against the sky and the smell of spiced tobacco wafts from the cafes under the bridge. Great place for having a beer and just watching the ferries plying up and down the Bosphorus.

*Getting a great view from the Galata Bridge.*

I have been back to Istanbul a couple of times since my Navy days and learnt one thing: never expect previous places visited to remain the same. Linda, my wife got thoroughly sick of me saying, "I'm sure that seventeenth century church wasn't there before." Istanbul was a case in point, as one of the places I took Linda back to; of course, hadn't changed in hundreds of years, but I swear that the Blue Mosque was in Taksim Square in 1962.

As I write this; the chair I'm sitting on sits on a carpet I bought on one of my return visits to Istanbul.

*A good deal all-round*

On the afternoon my wife and I were strolling through the
Grand Bazaar when a young man approached us and asked,
in perfect English, if he could have a word with us. He
explained that he was a student at Manchester University
and was currently on holiday helping his father run the
family carpet business. He added that he had been sent out
to try and persuade tourists to visit his father's shop and
would we consider just looking at the carpets, of course, no
obligation to buy, and this would show he had been doing
what his father had asked of him. I like to think that I am
somewhat streetwise and knew a scam when I saw one, but
for reasons I can't explain, we agreed and were lead up a side
street to a very small carpet shop. We met the father, who
called for apple tea and proceeded to show us some really
wonderful Turkish carpets. Of course, the inevitable
happened, and Linda fell in love with a beautiful traditional
rug. I put up all the arguments I could think of—it cost too
much, it's too big to get on the flight home, I don't have

enough money on me to pay for it, all to no avail. The price came down, it was folded small enough for hand luggage, and the student son knew of a cash machine in a bank just around the corner. It really was a lovely carpet, so I abandoned my poor wife to drink more tea with the old man, never thought that she may have been wrapped in a carpet and exported to someone's harem in my absence, and got the cash to pay for the goods

Looking at the carpet brings back lovely memories of Turkey and the carpet is still in everyday use and still looks great.

# Chapter 26

## Real Cruising and Working Bye.

Another P&O ship I briefly served on was The Orcades, a small passenger liner that had just started to cruise rather than transport people. A very short cruise starting from Southampton on 27th July and returning there on 10th August. I can't say that I enjoyed working on a cruise ship, it only went around the Mediterranean and it seem to me even in those days that it was becoming a bit like working in a hotel.

A shipping line I worked for but never sailed with was The New Zealand Shipping Company. In-between sailing with Union Castle and joining P&O I signed up on the New Zealand shipping Company ship, the "Rangitane". This was a cargo ship that carried some 30 passengers and was in the London Dock unloading its cargo of frozen lamb, it was also taking on new equipment and restocking catering items and wasn't due to sail for two weeks.

The New Zealand Shipping Company ran a passenger and cargo services between Great Britain and New Zealand between 1873 and 1973 when it was taken over by P&O. Working Bye is a term used when working on a ship before it sails. My job was to oversee the new stock of cutlery and crockery was unpacked, accounted for and restocked the restaurant and bars. Left more or less to my own devices was an easy time for me and working on the docks every day was a real experience. There was a pub that opened very early in the morning for the dockers and seamen to have a drink before or after work. I can't recall the name of the pub, could have been the Round House but it was just outside the dock gates and was the roughest, the barest and most uninviting place you have ever seem. There were no spirits or bottles to be seen and the only seating was long bare wooden tables and benches all sat on a stone floor. It was normally filled with Lascar seamen drinking pints of Guinness.

After a couple of weeks, I found out that the ship was due to sail on Christmas Eve rather than just after Christmas as was scheduled. Luckily as the ship was still in British waters I was able to sign off and spend Christmas at home

*The Rangitane*

*The Orcades*

# Chapter 27

## The Last Ship

I signed off Orcades in August 1962 and started to plan a voyage with my best schoolmate, Ron Parissien, but not everything in life turns out as you plan. Ron had just left the Royal Navy due to him losing his trigger finger and, being a gunner, he was able to leave before his service ended. The plan was for both of us to join the same ship and sail to more exotic places together. In the time I had been in the MN I had sailed many more sea miles than Ron and he wanted to experience real world travel. The first problem was that Ron could only get a job as deck crew on Shell tankers, so I duly applied to Shell and was taken on as a second steward or glorified catering officer on the M.S. Amastra. I joined the ship on 29 August 1962 at Immingham and immediately realised that I had made an almighty mistake and the worst part was that Ron had been assigned a different ship and was on his way to the Persian Gulf. When you signed ships articles in those days you could only sign off the vessel when it returned to British waters. Poor Ron spent the next eight months in the heat of the Gulf with only a Coke machine supplying something to drink. I on the other hand was very lucky in that the Amastra called in at Glasgow before docking in Liverpool to discharge oil, and one week after I had sailed from Immingham I signed off and took the Mersey ferry across to Liverpool for the first train back to my beloved London.

Five years after I left the Amastra it was mined in Nha Trang harbour, Vietnam when Viet Cong forces planted a limpet mine on the hull and it sank in the shallow water. I'm glad to say that none of the crew were injured. A report by the US Naval Authorities documents the whole tragic incident: -

At 00.10 hrs on 12<sup>th</sup> April, 1967 the 19,000-ton British Shell Oil Tanker M/V Amastra was holed by an explosive device while moored at anchor in Nha Trang harbour, Vietnam. The Amastra was preparing to off load aviation fuel for US military aircraft when the explosion ripped open a six-foot hole at the waterline. The crew of the Amastra were transferred to Army landing craft and spent the night at the American Army Officers quarters at camp John McDermott in Nha Trang.

*It's sad to see my old cabin from the photos of the half-sunk ship.*

*Amastra after the bomb April 1st 1967*

Leaving Shell was the end of my Merchant Navy career and I couldn't think of what would come next. Unfortunately, I still didn't know what I wanted to do after I left school but I knew that this would not be my end of ocean travel.

# Chapter 28

## Salford Docks & Seaman Duties

After leaving the Merchant Navy in 1962 and several years in a variety of occupations I thought my days of big ships were over, but no. In 1975 I joined HM Immigration Service and was stationed at Manchester Airport; this Office was responsible for the movement of ships and men at Salford Docks. Shipping agents would inform us of the arrival of their ships into Salford Docks and one officer was assigned to attend and check out the crew etc. It wasn't long before I was on Seaman Officer control and duly drove down to Salford to board the ship.

My first ship was an old general cargo vessel of Polish origin, the dreaded "Wolin" It was built in 1959 of 1519 tons and could take up to 8 passengers, however in the 10 years or so I dealt with the Wolin I can't remember a single passenger. Along with the Russian ships we also had to deal with the Wolin which presented a big problem-their hospitality.

A lot of the time the work was carried out in collaboration with Special Branch (SB) and as interesting as this work was, it was fraught with danger—the danger of getting blind drunk. The hospitality of those nations is legendary, none more so than with their seafaring men, and on entering the captain's cabin the cry was always "Welcome—we will have vodka." Not wanting to offend, the offer to toast our two nations was usually taken up, and sometimes with devastating results, like the time an Immigration Officer, who will be nameless, dropped his official case containing all his stamps and a set of books containing hundreds of names of interest, into Salford Docks, and as far as I know it still remains beneath several metres of water. On one such seaman duty I had to visit a small Greek coaster that was docked at Cadishead, near Warrington. The ship was moored some distance from the road and so myself and an SB Officer set off across the railway lines in the dock area to this rusty old coaster. Halfway there, we met a lady going in the opposite direction who could only be described as looking very rough and to be honest, past her best. The SB Officer had in the past been part of the vice squad with the Greater Manchester Police and recognised the lady as being well-known to him. He greeted her with a cheery "Hello, Mary, have you had a good night?". With a big smile on her face, she told us that she had had to service the whole crew but had earned a small fortune. Opening her purse, she showed us a couple of handfuls of Greek Drachma notes which probably amounted to less than £5. I felt extremely sorry for Mary but alas, there wasn't much we could do except give the captain and crew a thorough vetting.

Being stationed at Manchester Airport meant that we also covered Liverpool Airport when required and provided relief at the Liverpool Docks. I spent 6 weeks working from Liverpool Airport and got to know the docks fairly well. The docks weren't the busy place that I saw very briefly in the 60s but busy enough to get us out of the office and visiting various small cargo ships every day. The highlight of the day was to return to the Immigration Office and go out to lunch to The Slaughter House, no not a place they kill animals but one of Liverpool's oldest pubs.

*The Wolin in all its rusty glory*

*In the late seventies this old pub in Fenwick Street still had sawdust on the floor and a great atmosphere.*

# Chapter 29

## A Passenger at Last

In recent years I have been on a number of cruises, thankfully as a passenger, sailing with Holland America, Norwegian Line, Princess, Celebrity, Royal Caribbean, Cunard, and P&O. On one of the trips with P&O, I approached the Purser's Office (now sadly called the Customer Service desk) to ask, as a former employee of the line, if I could see the crew's quarters. A day later I received a phone call to say I had been assigned an assistant customer service officer to show me around below deck. To say that I was surprised during the inspection was the understatement of the year. I was totally unprepared for the facilities and conditions I was shown. Several crew bars, lounge areas with a large LED TV screen, single and double cabins, a swimming pool, and, to top it all, a jacuzzi. It was light years away from my four-in-a-cabin and very small crew mess. Life on the ocean wave has certainly changed a bit! One thing that is hard to get one's head around is the statistics of a present-day cruise in terms of numbers. A ship of some 90,000 tons uses on average 15,225 pool towels on a seven-day cruise, sheets required on the same sailing: 11,600, bars of soap used in a year: 5,000,000, and the number of chocolates placed on pillows in a year: 15,000,000. Useless stats, I know, but no less impressive.

After some years of happily cruising the sea on big ships I was getting a bit tired of hundreds of people so I thought I'd try something a little smaller and at a gentler pace - river cruising, and what a lovely change. Budapest to Nuremberg via Vienna, what could be nicer, it was magnificent and the sights along the way were breath-taking. This Blue Danube cruise was all I expected it to be and more, peaceful and serene as you glide past castles, churches and that wonderful countryside.

*River cruising at its best*

My next small ship was ever smaller, a cruise in a motor yacht around the Croatian coast and this time the ship took only 38 passengers rather than hundreds. After all these years I had found my sort of cruising, always near the coast and in a beautiful small port every night, heaven.

*Just leaving Dubrovnik the lovely Infinity*

As a cruise passenger I have seen a lot more of the world, bits I hadn't visited in the Merchant Navy and have now visited most of the Caribbean Islands as well as Russia and Scandinavia. I'm so glad to say that given the size of modern cruise liners I no longer seem to succumb to sea sickness and after 50 years I think I can say that I have finally got my sea legs.

*A passenger at last*

Printed in Great Britain
by Amazon

42362834R00071